JONNY LAMBERT'S
Bear and Bird
Find a
Footprint

DK

CAN YOU SPOT?

Ladybug

Wren

WHAT TO SPOT!

Use the "CAN YOU SPOT?" panels on every page to discover hidden forest secrets, as you join Bear and Bird on their wonderful adventure.

Where is the slimy slug?

CAN YOU HELP?

Can you help Bear and Bird find what they are looking for?

Fox

WHOSE FOOTPRINT?

Get to know the footprints of different animals, so you can find out who's been passing by.

For everyone looking for an adventure —Jonny Lambert

JONNY LAMBERT'S

Bear and Bird
Find a
Footprint

DK

Bear and Bird were very excited.
The rain had finally passed and the
sun was warming the air.

Best of all, they had a picnic ready
to share with their friends, in a beautiful
spot nearby.

Can you find
the little wren?

"We should be on our way," chirped Bird.

"I agree," replied Bear, "I can't wait to see everyone. And my tummy's rumbling, too!"

CAN YOU SPOT?

Bumblebee

Pine cone

Butterfly

Bluebell

Wren

Buttercup

CAN YOU SPOT?

Woodpecker

Honeysuckle

Warbler

Beetle

Squirrel

They hadn't walked far before Bear spotted some muddy footprints leading away from the path. He bent down for a closer look.

"Um, I don't recognize these!"

Who is pecking noisily on the tree?

Bird flew back to look at the prints, too.

"Well, they're not ours. I wonder
who they belong to?"

Bear and Bird's footprints are very
different from the ones they've found.
Who could they belong to?

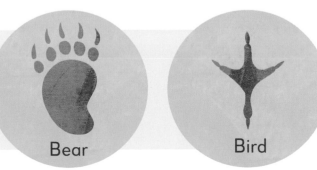

Bear

Bird

"Look!" Bird cried. "The footprints go this way... come on!"

Excited by their discovery, Bird flew on ahead.

She really wanted to find the owner of these muddy prints.

Where is the slimy slug?

Bear sighed. His tummy rumbled louder than ever. But he scampered after Bird.

"I hope they stop soon!"

CAN YOU SPOT?

Ladybug

Owl

Acorns

Slug

Before long they found themselves at the old oak tree, and behind it was Fox!

"Are these muddy footprints yours?" asked Bear.

"No, they don't belong to me," replied Fox.

What is climbing on the tree?

"But, maybe Moose might know."

"Okay!" cried Bear, "but let's be quick. Then we can have our picnic!"

CAN YOU SPOT?

Spider

Fungi

Lizard

Fox

A fox's footprints are like a dog's, but they are longer and narrower.

Bear, Bird, and Fox found Moose, next. He was staring at the ground and looking puzzled.

"Do you know who made these footprints?" he asked.

Who is flying high in the sky?

"We thought you'd tell us," sighed Bear.

"Well, they aren't mine," laughed Moose.
"But if we find who made them,
they can come to our picnic!"

Moose

The hard part at the end of a moose's foot is called a hoof. Each hoof has two large toes.

CAN YOU SPOT?

Berries

Swallow

Moth

Snail

Wild rose

CAN YOU SPOT?

Kingfisher

Reeds

Newt

Primrose

Smelt

At the edge of a pond, the footprints stopped.

Bear was confused. "Hello, Frog!
Did you see who made these muddy prints?"

Frog shook her head.

"I've been swimming in the pond all day!
But look, the footprints carry on this way."

What is swimming under Frog's lily pad?

Frogs have webbed feet that help them climb and swim.

Frog

Who is sitting
on Bear's
picnic basket?

Frog joined them as they followed the prints.

"The marks are difficult to spot under
all these leaves!" exclaimed Fox.

"Look!" cried Bear, pointing at the ground. "The prints are all mixed up here. What do you think their owner was doing?"

"They were looking for food," replied Bird.

Bear's tummy gurgled loudly.
"Well, I'd like to eat our food soon!"

CAN YOU SPOT?

Birch leaf

Chestnut

Mouse

Nest

Sycamore seeds

Maple leaf

CAN YOU SPOT?

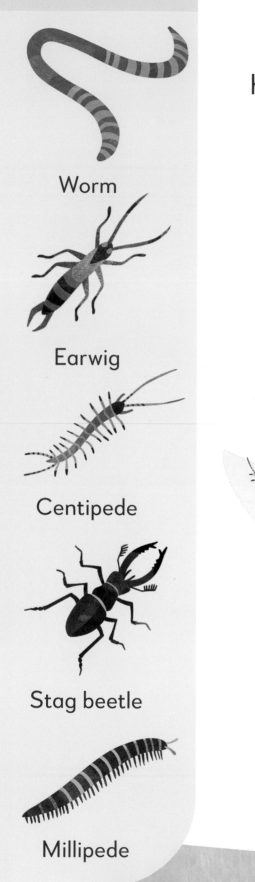

Worm

Earwig

Centipede

Stag beetle

Millipede

As Fox followed the footprints into a
hollowed-out log, there was a sudden loud snort.

"Hey, what are you doing?
This is my home!" cried Squirrel.

Squirrel popped out, very upset.

Both Bear and Bird apologized.
"We are sorry to disturb you, but is there
anyone else inside your log?"

Squirrel

A squirrel's paws
have very strong
claws for digging
and climbing.

What is crawling
on Fox's tail?

CAN YOU SPOT?

Feather

Snail shell

Blackberries

Termite

Hazelnuts

"No, there isn't," said Squirrel,
"But I'll help you look in every
hole, nook, and crack."

So, they lifted every mossy rock,
and turned over every stone.

"There's no one here!" Bear exclaimed,
"Only ants, termites, and
a few slimy snail trails."

"Come on... let's keep
following the prints!" urged Bird.

CAN YOU SPOT?

Fern

Ants

Beetle wing

Eggshell

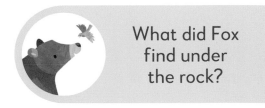

What did Fox
find under
the rock?

Where is the
honeybee hive?

The footprints led them to a cave,
and Bear popped his head inside.

"Yoohoo!" he bellowed. "Is there anyone in here?"

Bats fluttered out, disturbed by Bear's big booming voice.

"It's very dark in there," said Moose. "And a bit smelly, too!"

"Look!" yapped Fox. "I found the footprints—they go this way."

CAN YOU SPOT?

Honeybee

Hive

Bat

Fungus

Ivy

CAN YOU SPOT?

Grasshopper

Jackrabbit

Wheat grass

Daisy

Poppy

Hurrying on, they scampered through a wheatfield. Suddenly, rabbits ran in all directions, shouting, "Fox!"

"I'm not chasing you," said Fox.
"I just wanted to ask if you know
who made these tracks?"

Rabbit

Rabbits have
very furry feet.
Their strong
claws help them
dig burrows.

"We do!" replied one brave rabbit.
"They went that way, to the river bank!"

Who is sitting
by the old
tree stump?

CAN YOU SPOT?

Dragonfly

Water skater

Goose

Salmon

Rushing to the river bank, they discovered
Duck quacking happily on a rock.

"Hello, Duck!" called Bear. "We've been following these footprints... are they yours?"

After another loud quack, Duck replied, "Yes, they belong to me!"

"Hooray!" They all cheered. "Come and join our picnic."

Who is leaping out of the water?

Duck

Ducks have webbed feet, shaped like paddles. These help them move through the water.

"This picnic is fun!" cheered Fox
and Moose. "Thank you, Bear and Bird."

Bear handed Duck another cookie.
"Did you enjoy your walk today?"

"I did," replied Duck. "And I saw lots of wonderful things in the forest, too."

"Bear," chirped Bird, "can you remember what we saw on our forest adventure?"

What else did you see in the forest?

Honeysuckle

Berries

Lizard

Bumblebee

Pine cone

Fungi

Swallow

Ladybug

Butterfly

Woodpecker

Owl

Moth

Primrose

Bluebell

Warbler

Acorns

Snail

Smelt

Wren

Squirrel

Slug

Kingfisher

Birch leaf

Buttercup

Chestnut

Beetle

Spider

Wild rose

Reeds

Mouse

Newt

Nest

Hazelnuts

Bat

Daisy

Sycamore
seeds

Stag beetle

Fern

Honeybee

Poppy

Maple leaf

Millipede

Ants

Hive

Dragonfly

Worm

Feather

Beetle wing

Grasshopper

Water skater

Earwig

Snail shell

Eggshell

Jackrabbit

Goose

Centipede

Blackberries

Fungus

Ivy

Wheat grass

Salmon

Termite

Illustrated and written by Jonny Lambert
Editor Kat Teece
Designer Eleanor Bates
US Senior Editor Shannon Beatty
Managing Art Editor Diane Peyton Jones
Publishing Manager Francesca Young
Creative Director Mabel Chan
Publishing Director Sarah Larter
Production Editor Dragana Puvacic
Producer Inderjit Bhullar

First American Edition, 2023
Published in the United States by DK Publishing
1745 Broadway, 20th Floor, New York, NY 10019

Copyright © 2023 Dorling Kindersley Limited
DK, a Division of Penguin Random House LLC
23 24 25 26 27 10 9 8 7 6 5 4 3 2 1
001–336865–Sep/2023

A catalog record for this book
is available from the Library of Congress.
ISBN 978-0-7440-8581-5

DK books are available at special discounts when purchased
in bulk for sales promotions, premiums, fund-raising, or
educational use. For details, contact: DK Publishing Special
Markets, 1745 Broadway, 20th Floor, New York, NY 10019
SpecialSales@dk.com

Printed and bound in China

For the curious
www.dk.com

MIX
Paper | Supporting
responsible forestry
FSC™ C018179

This book was made with Forest
Stewardship Council™ certified
paper – one small step in DK's
commitment to a sustainable future.
**For more information go to
www.dk.com/our-green-pledge**